j
796.2
SAYCO

14 x 7/07

THE ULTIMATE YO-YO BOOK

20 Great Tricks and Tips!

WITHDRAWN

By Larry Sayco

Illustrated by Brian Floca

For my older brother Louis,
the real champion of the family.

Text copyright © 1998 by Larry Sayco. Illustrations cop,
All rights reserved. Published by Grosset & Dunla
Penguin Putnam Books for Young Readers, New York.
is a trademark of Grosset & Dunlap,
Published simultaneously in Canada. Printed in
Library of Congress Catalog Card Number: 97-

ISBN 0-448-41840-1   C D E F G H i

TABLE OF CONTENTS

TEN TIPS FOR GETTING STARTED

1. Make sure your yo-yo isn't too light. Use one that weighs at least an ounce.

2. Use a plain yo-yo—not one that lights up, whistles, hums, recites a poem, or anything fancy.

3. Don't take your yo-yo apart (unless it's a special yo-yo made to be taken apart).

4. Unwind the string and stand the yo-yo on the floor in front of you. Then have a grown-up cut the string even with your chest. The string will be a little long, but when you tie a finger loop, it should be just right—at your bellybutton.

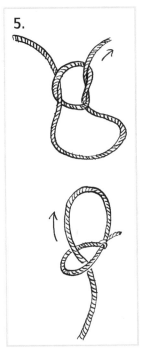

5. Tie a small loop at the end of the string, and pull part of the string through the loop each time you yo-yo for an easy slipknot.

6. Place the slipknot loop on your middle finger. Beginners should put the loop right next to their hand. Better players should keep the loop between the first and second knuckle.

7. A slipknot fits tightly over your finger while you are playing, but opens up easily when you want to take it off. If the string hurts or stops your blood flow, take a break for a while. Or wrap a Band-Aid around your finger and put the loop over the Band-Aid.

8. Read all the directions for a trick before you try to do it.

9. You can't do the hard tricks until you learn the easy ones. Do each trick one step at a time.

10. Last but not least, always BE CAREFUL when using a yo-yo, even if you're alone. If you're doing the tricks in front of other people, make sure they know to stand back!

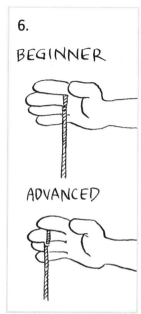

6.

BEGINNER

ADVANCED

10.

How Knot to Yo-Yo

All yo-yo players, from beginners to pros, have trouble with knots. Here are some tips to help you.

- ⦿ DON'T swing or dangle the yo-yo hoping the knot will undo itself.

- ⦿ DON'T pull on both ends of the string, or on the yo-yo and the string. This can make things worse.

- ⦿ NEVER use a knife to undo the knot.

- ⦿ If the knot is in the yo-yo, open up a paper clip and use it to pick open the knot. (Have an adult help you.)

- ⦿ If the knot is only in the length of the string, look at it closely to see how it's knotted. Then try to pick the knot open. Remember—knots require patience!

One last tip:

When you buy a yo-yo, pick up some extra string. If your string breaks, wears out, or is so badly knotted that you have to cut it, you'll be ready. Follow the manufacturer's directions for replacing the string.

KINKS

If the yo-yo string twists too tight, it will form tiny beads, known as kinks or pig-tailing. This is easy to fix. Just let the yo-yo drop to the end of the string and untwist itself.

TAKING CARE OF THE STRING

After eating, always wash your hands before you play with your yo-yo again, even if you've only had a snack like chips or cookies. Food grease on the string can sometimes make the yo-yo slip. If the string does get dirty, remove it. Ask a grown-up to pin it to one of your white shirts, and toss it in the laundry machine. When the string dries, it will look and feel like new!

WINDING THE YO-YO

Wrap each turn by hand. If you are left-handed, wrap the string toward you. If you are right-handed, wrap it away from you. If the string doesn't catch, try this: pinch the string about 2 inches above the yo-yo. Wind with the string slack until it starts to catch.

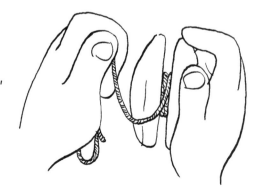

SINGLE AND DOUBLE AXLE LOOPS

Inside the groove of a yo-yo, the string is looped around the axle. The string can be either single looped or double looped around the axle. Beginners sometimes find it easier to learn on a yo-yo that is double looped, but they soon have to switch over to a single loop. You can't do any of the sleeper tricks with the yo-yo double looped.

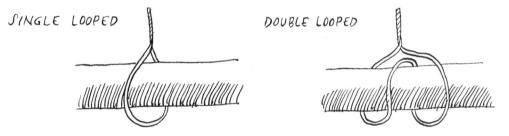

SINGLE LOOPED   DOUBLE LOOPED

If your yo-yo is double looped, hold the string tightly and untwist the yo-yo to the left (counter clockwise) until you see two separate strings. Open the space between the strings and pass the yo-yo through it. Now your yo-yo is single looped. You may have to tighten the string by twisting the yo-yo to the right (clockwise).

DOWN AND UP

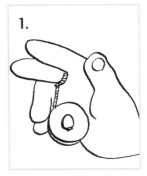

1. Hold the yo-yo in your hand like a ball. Your palm should be down and about even with your bellybutton, but not touching your body.

2. Open your hand and let the yo-yo drop toward the floor. As soon as you open your hand, say "Yo-Yo."

3. After the second "Yo," smoothly lift your yo-yo hand up about 3 or 4 inches. You'll feel a snap when the yo-yo reaches the bottom of the string, and because of your tug, the yo-yo will climb up the opposite side of the string.

4. When the yo-yo reaches the top of the string, close your hand quickly to catch it.

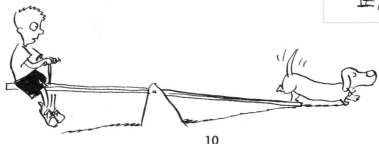

DOWN AND UP TROUBLE TIPS

Problem	Cause	What to Do
Yo-yo wobbles sideways.	Yo-yo isn't heavy enough.	Until you get a heavier one, tape a penny on the center of each side of the yo-yo.
Yo-yo keeps going sideways, and it's not the weight of the yo-yo.	You're pushing the yo-yo down when you open your hand.	Open your hand gently but quickly to let the yo-yo fall to Mother Earth.
Yo-yo goes down okay, but doesn't come up all the way, or doesn't come up at all.	Your tug timing is slightly off.	Instead of saying "Yo-Yo," try counting "One, Two." Open on "One" and pull up on "Two."
Yo-yo returns to your hand, but with a hand full of spaghetti (unwound string).	You're grabbing the yo-yo too soon.	Wait until the yo-yo touches your hand before you snap it shut.

THE BOUNCING YO-YO

This trick is based on the basic Down and Up.
It's a little harder, but fun practice!

1.   Open your hand and let the yo-yo fall.

2.   Tug up on the string, but when the yo-yo
returns to your hand, don't try to catch it.

3.   Keep your hand flat and give the yo-yo
a gentle pat to make it go back down.

4.   Repeat until you feel like catching it.

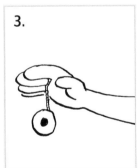

**Once you get the timing down on this trick,
it's almost like bouncing a ball. You can do it
forever—or at least until the string breaks or
your finger falls off!**

Now be a show-off!

- Try the Bouncing Yo-Yo standing on only one foot.

- Try the Bouncing Yo-Yo with your eyes closed. No peeking!

- Try the Bouncing Yo-Yo with your eyes closed and standing on one foot. If you can do this, you're really good. Most people can't do this even without the yo-yo!

THE FORWARD PASS

Practice this trick without the yo-yo a couple of times to get the feel of it.

1. Pretend you are about to throw a bowling ball. If you're right-handed, stand with your right foot slightly out in front. If you're left-handed, stand with your left foot slightly out in front.

2. Put your yo-yo hand, palm up, as far back as you can. Keep your wrist curled.

3. Swing your arm forward, uncurling your wrist. Let go of the yo-yo when your hand is even with your forward toe. This will send the yo-yo in front of you at an angle.

4. Once the yo-yo is completely out of your hand, turn your hand so your palm faces the ceiling again.

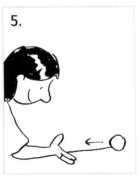

5. The yo-yo will spin to the end of the string, reverse itself, and return to your hand, where you can catch it.

FORWARD PASS TROUBLE TIPS

Problem	Cause	What to Do
Yo-yo twists when it leaves your hand.	You're twisting your hand too soon.	Make sure the yo-yo is completely out of your hand before the twist. Try counting again. Throw on "One," and twist on "Two."
You can't catch the yo-yo on its return.	You're throwing either too hard or too soft.	A fast throw can be tough to catch. A soft throw won't make it all the way back. Adjust the speed of your throw.
Yo-yo goes out straight, but returns too high to catch.	You're releasing the yo-yo too late.	Remember to let go of the yo-yo when your hand passes your forward toe.

See how many Forward Passes in a row you can throw!

15

> **IMPORTANT NOTE!**
> **Read Before Going On!**
> From now on the tricks get a little harder. At this point, if you've been wearing the finger loop at the base of your middle finger, move it up between the joints (see picture, page 5). This will give you more control. It may feel funny at first, but soon you'll get used to it.

LOOP THE LOOP

A single Loop the Loop is sometimes tough for beginners to learn, but it is the basis for all other looping tricks.

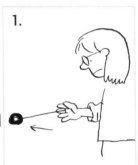

1. Stand and throw the yo-yo the same way you did for the Forward Pass.

2. When the yo-yo comes back, don't catch it. Instead, direct the yo-yo between your arm and your body, making a circle with your wrist. This is almost like waving someone to come back, except you follow all the way around with a swift snap.

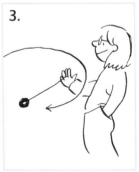

3. The yo-yo will pass very close to your stomach, then go back out away from you, making a loop.

LOOP THE LOOP TIPS

- If you are having trouble, re-read the directions carefully.

- Remove the yo-yo from your finger and practice the wrist motion until you get the hang of it.

- DON'T be scared of the yo-yo.

- Try doing the Forward Pass several times in a row. When you see a really excellent one coming back at you, GO FOR IT!

- DON'T give up. Keep trying until you get the hang of it. You're going to feel proud for doing this difficult trick by yourself!

Once you can do a perfect loop every time, try for two in a row. Then three or four! See how many you can do without stopping.

> **IMPORTANT NOTE!**
> Before doing the rest of the tricks in this book, make sure your yo-yo is single looped (see page 9). Try a few simple tricks with the yo-yo single looped to get used to the feel of it before going on.

THE SLEEPER

1. Curl your hand, bend your elbow, and make a muscle like Popeye, but with your arm in front of you.

2. Give your hand, fingers, wrist, and arm a downward whipping motion—like you're shaking water off your hand—throwing the yo-yo out and in front of you.

3. As you throw the yo-yo, lift your hand 3 or 4 inches, then turn it so the palm faces the ground. If you do this right, the yo-yo will spin or "sleep" at the bottom of the string.

4. Give the string a quick upward tug to make the yo-yo return to you.

5. Catch it.

SLEEPER TROUBLE TIPS

Problem	Cause	What to Do
Yo-yo sleeps but won't come back up.	String is too loose.	Tighten by unwinding the yo-yo, then twisting it to the right (clockwise) about 20 times.
Yo-yo won't sleep. It returns as soon as you throw it.	String is too tight.	Loosen string by unwinding the yo-yo and letting it untwist to the left (counter clockwise).
	OR	
	You're throwing the yo-yo wrong.	Throw the yo-yo out and just leave it there. Don't tug or jerk the string at all.
Yo-yo slants to one side.	You're turning your hand too soon.	Make sure the yo-yo is completely out of your hand before you turn it.
	OR	
	Yo-yo isn't spinning fast enough.	Try throwing harder with more of a snap.
	OR	
	You're slanting the throw.	Practice in a room with straight lines on the floor. Stand with your feet parallel to the lines. Then throw the yo-yo so that it also spins parallel to those lines.

Lots of tricks are based on sleepers. Here are some fun ones to try. They're especially good to show off in front of your friends or family. Just a hint, though—when doing tricks in front of people, always tell them the name of the trick before you do it!

SPANK THE BABY

1. Throw a good, fast, straight sleeper.

2. While it's sleeping, say, "Naughty baby."

3. Then use your free hand to slap or spank the back of your yo-yo hand. That should be enough of a jerk to make the yo-yo return.

4. Catch it.

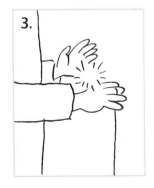

When you do a sleeping trick, make sure the yo-yo is spinning straight and fast enough to finish the trick. If it isn't, catch it, or it might die in the middle!

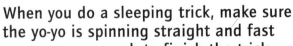

SPANK THE BABY TWICE

This looks better if you do Spank the Baby first.

1. Throw a good, fast, straight sleeper.

2. With your free hand, spank the baby twice, but not hard enough to bring the yo-yo back up. Say, "I spanked the baby twice, but he didn't wake up."

3. Make a fist with your free hand and poke it hard upward into the palm of your yo-yo hand. Say, "So I gave him a poke in the tummy!"

4. When the yo-yo comes back up, catch it.

THE KARATE CHOP

1. Start just like Spank the Baby.

2. Instead of giving your hand a spank, give the knuckles of your yo-yo hand a karate chop, yelling, "Hi-YA!"

3. When the yo-yo comes up, catch it.

Don't overdo it. Remember, it's your own hand you're karate chopping!

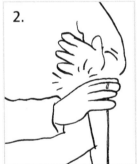

THE BOW AND ARROW

1. Throw another good, fast sleeper.

2. While the yo-yo is sleeping, lift your yo-yo hand high, so the middle part of the string is at eye level, but away from your body.

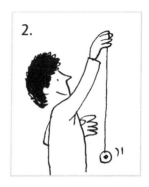

3. Squint like you're taking aim. Then with your free hand, pluck the middle of the string as if it were a guitar.

4. As soon as you pluck the string, the yo-yo should come up. Catch it, and say, "Bull's-eye!"

THE BUZZ SAW

1. Crumple up a piece of scrap paper and put it on the floor in front of you.

2. Throw a fast sleeper.

3. Lightly skim the spinning yo-yo over the top of the paper. You will hear it make a buzzing noise.

4. Before it spins out, give the string a tug and catch the yo-yo.

Don't be a litter bug. Throw away or recycle the paper when you're done!

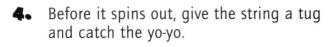

THE CUCKOO CLOCK

1. Throw a good sleeper.

2. Hold your yo-yo hand in one place, and make the yo-yo swing back and forth like the pendulum of a large clock. Say, "Tick-Tock, Tick-Tock."

3. Bring the yo-yo back up. When you catch it say, "Cuckoo!"

See how many times you can swing the yo-yo back and forth, and still catch it.

SEVEN-UP

1. Throw a real hard sleeper.

2. When it starts to spin, count "1, 2, 3, 4, 5, 6, 7, and up!"

3. When you say "up!" tug the string and catch the yo-yo.

At first you may have to count fast, but as you get better, you'll be able to count even higher than 7!

TAKE A HIKE

1. Throw a fast sleeper.

2. Walk a few steps forward, turn around, and come back to where you started.

3. Bring the yo-yo up and catch it.

See how far you can go and come back, while still making a smooth catch at the end. Just be careful not to bump into anything!

WALK THE DOG

1. Start with a very fast, straight sleeper.

2. Move your yo-yo hand directly above the yo-yo. This should stop its swinging.

3. When the string is straight up and down, gently lower the yo-yo to the floor, letting it barely skim over the ground.

4. The spin of the yo-yo will move it across the floor. Guide it with your yo-yo hand.

5. Tug the string to bring the yo-yo back up. Then catch it.

For fun, find a few friends and hold a Walk the Dog race. Who can go the farthest? It doesn't count if the yo-yo stops or you don't catch it with all the string wound up inside.

WHAT ABOUT ME?

WALK THE DOG TROUBLE TIPS

Problem	Cause	What to Do
Yo-yo touches the floor and comes up immediately.	String is too tight.	Loosen the string (see page 19).
	.... OR	
	Yo-yo is hitting the floor too hard or at an angle.	The string must be **straight** up and down before you **gently** lower the yo-yo.

Take care of your yo-yo!

◉ DON'T walk your yo-yo over cement. Cement can chew up the edges.

◉ DON'T walk it over the ground outside. Pebbles, sand, or dirt might get stuck in the groove. Blades of grass can get caught between the string and the axle.

◉ DON'T walk your yo-yo through a puddle. Water is very bad for yo-yos.

The best place to walk your yo-yo is over a wood floor, or a short, not so shaggy carpet.

FIRE HYDRANT ZIGZAG

You'll need six empty soda cans for this trick.

1. Stand the soda cans in a line. They should be 6 inches apart.

2. Pretend each can is a fire hydrant, then Walk the Dog, zigzagging through the space between each can.

3. See how many cans you go by without knocking any over. (If the yo-yo moves or touches a can, that's okay, as long as the can stays standing.)

4. Bring the yo-yo up and catch it.

HIT OR MISS

You'll need one clean, dry, empty soda can for this trick.

1. Stand the soda can up beside you.

2. Throw a good, hard sleeper and let the yo-yo swing toward the can.

3. Try to make the swinging yo-yo miss the can as it swings forward, but knock over the can on the return swing.

4. Bring the yo-yo back up and catch it.

Seems easy, right? It's harder than you think.

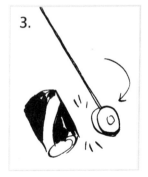

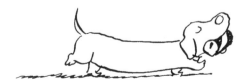

HALF MOON

1. Hold the yo-yo as you would for a sleeper, but with your arm to the side.

2. Make sure there is nothing near you on that side.

3. Curl your wrist as much as you can to start, then uncurl it as you throw a sleeper sideways.

4. When the yo-yo reaches the end of the string, swing it in a half-circle in front of you.

5. Give the string a tug when the yo-yo reaches the height of your other shoulder.

6. Hold your yo-yo hand palm up and catch the yo-yo.

HALF MOON TROUBLE TIPS

Problem	Cause	What to Do
Yo-yo won't sleep.	String is too tight.	Loosen string (see page 19).
	·········· OR ··········	
	You're throwing wrong.	Throw the yo-yo both high and sideways.
You have trouble catching the yo-yo after the trick.	You're throwing the yo-yo too hard or too soft.	Adjust the speed of the throw.
	·········· OR ··········	
	Your catching hand is in the wrong position.	Stand with your yo-yo hand about waist high, palm facing the yo-yo, knuckles toward the ground.

33

EATING SPAGHETTI

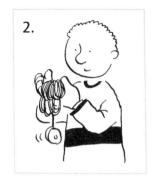

1. Throw a fast, straight sleeper.

2. While the yo-yo is sleeping, bunch up the string with both hands to within 3 inches of the yo-yo.

3. Put all the bunched-up string in your yo-yo hand, leaving your other hand free.

4. Pretend you are sprinkling cheese and sauce on your handful of spaghetti, then hold it in front of your mouth.

5. Let go of all the string while making a slurping sound. If the yo-yo is spinning fast enough, the string will disappear into the yo-yo, and everyone will think you slurped up all the spaghetti in just one gulp!

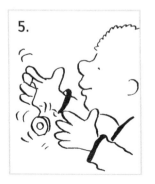

6. Catch the yo-yo, then rub your belly. Delicious!

THE TUMBLING TOWER

You'll need four empty soda cans for this trick.

1. Stack the cans, one on top of the other.

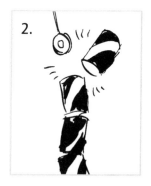

2. Throw a hard sleeper, then swing the yo-yo, trying to knock the top can off the tower.

3. With each swing, try to knock only one can off the tower.

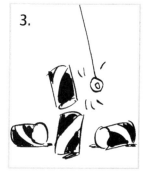

4. When you've knocked over the last can, tug on the string and catch the yo-yo.

Try this trick with a friend—take turns knocking a can off the tower. (Be careful not to hit each other!)

YO-YO BOWLING

You'll need ten clean, empty cans to go bowling!

1. Set up the cans in a triangle, like the pins at a bowling alley.

2. Stand about 2 or 3 feet in front of the first can.

3. Throw a straight sleeper and gently remove the finger loop from your finger.

4. Lower the yo-yo to the ground as if you were Walking the Dog.

5. When it starts to "walk," let go of the string.

See how many cans you knock over!

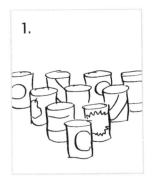

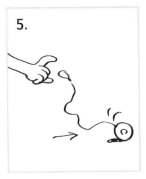

THE CREEPER

1. Throw a fast sleeper and let it swing as in the Cuckoo Clock.

2. When the yo-yo swings out in front of you as far as it can go, squat down quickly and put your yo-yo hand, palm down, on the floor. The yo-yo should sleep on the floor in front of you.

3. Give the string a quick tug to make the yo-yo creep across the floor to your hand. Then catch it.

Here's a tip—keep the yo-yo as close to the floor as possible when swinging it out. If the yo-yo is higher than a foot off the floor, don't try the trick. Just catch it and try again.

2.

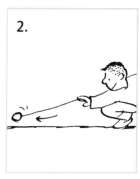

3.

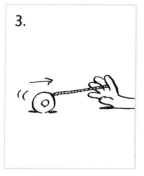

THE STATUE OF LIBERTY

You'll need one empty soda can for this patriotic trick. Make sure the can is clean and very dry, or you may end up with sticky soda running down your arm. Yuck!

1. Hold the can upside down in your free hand.

2. Throw a fast sleeper on the <u>side</u>, not out front. Make sure the flat side of the yo-yo is toward you.

3. Let the yo-yo swing once. As it comes up, try to land the yo-yo—still spinning—on top of the can.

4. While whistling, humming, or singing a few lines of your favorite patriotic song, raise the can with the yo-yo on it above your head. Stand in a Statue of Liberty pose.

5. To catch the yo-yo, push the can up toward the ceiling, then quickly pull the can out of the way.

6. Catch the yo-yo in your yo-yo hand.

STATUE OF LIBERTY TROUBLE TIPS

Problem	Cause	What to Do
Yo-yo bounces off the can instead of landing there.	You're holding the can too stiffly.	Relax! As the yo-yo drops down on the can, lower the can a little to absorb the shock.
Yo-yo spins a short time on the can, but then jerks back to your yo-yo hand.	Too much slack in the string.	While the yo-yo is spinning on the can, keep the string sort of tight.
After you do the trick, you can't catch the yo-yo.	Yo-yo hand is in wrong position.	Catch the yo-yo overhand, not underhand. The tip of your yo-yo finger should point to the ceiling, not the ground.

AROUND THE WORLD

1. Start the trick as a Forward Pass, but swing your arm a little higher in front of you, stopping when your hand is about at the height of your shoulder. (Don't turn your hand as you usually would for a Forward Pass.)

2. The yo-yo should move up and back, making a large circle outside your arm.

3. When the yo-yo completes the circle, turn your hand around and give the yo-yo a tug to wake it up.

4. Catch the yo-yo.

AROUND THE WORLD TROUBLE TIPS

Problem	Cause	What to Do
When you throw the yo-yo out, it just comes right back.	String is too tight.	Loosen string (see page 19).
	·········· OR ··········	
	You're throwing wrong.	It only starts like a Forward Pass. Aim more for the ground as you swiftly uncurl your wrist toward the sky.

Don't try doing more than one Around the World at a time. If you try for more than one orbit on a single throw, the string may snap. Then it would be time to start saving for a new yo-yo!

41

THE BUNNY HOP

1. Throw a fast, hard sleeper, but don't turn your hand as you normally would.

2. While the yo-yo sleeps, place the elbow of your yo-yo hand in front of the string.

3. With the string touching the back of your arm, bring your hand down and lift your elbow to the height of your shoulder.

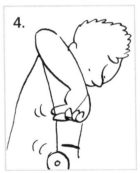

4. Curl the wrist of your yo-yo hand so your fingers are 2 or 3 inches from the string and give the string a quick pluck with your forefinger and thumb.

5. The yo-yo should wake up, run up the string, hop over your arm, and begin to go down the opposite side.

6. Let the yo-yo reach the bottom of the string, then bring it up and catch it.

Keep your eye on the yo-yo at all times!

THE BUNNY HOP TROUBLE TIPS

Problem	Cause	What to Do
Yo-yo comes up when you put it behind your elbow.	String is too tight.	Loosen string (see page 19).
You can't find the string to pluck it.	You're standing too straight and looking forward.	When you're ready to pluck, twist your head down and almost under your armpit, so you can see the string.
You pluck the string but the yo-yo won't come up.	String is too loose.	Tighten the string by twisting the yo-yo (see page 19).
	····· OR ·····	
	You're not plucking hard enough.	Give it a good banjo twang.
You can't catch the yo-yo when the trick is done.	You're trying to catch it at the wrong time.	Don't try to catch the yo-yo as it comes over your arm. Let it go back down first, and catch it when it comes up.

ROCK THE BABY

Time to learn the most popular trick in yo-yo history!

1. Throw a fast sleeper.

2. With your free hand, grab the string about halfway down.

3. Reach your yo-yo hand below your free hand and pinch the string between your index finger and thumb.

4. Reverse your catch by putting your top hand down and your bottom hand up.

5. Open your fist without losing the string. The string should take the shape of a triangle.

6. If your yo-yo is still spinning fast and straight, swing the yo-yo in and out of the cradle.

7. On the last swing, release the string from both hands. The yo-yo should come back to you all wound up.

ROCK THE BABY TIPS AND TRICKS

Problem	Cause	What to Do
Yo-yo comes up when you grab it.	String is too tight.	Loosen string (see page 19).
	···· OR ····	
	Your grabbing motions are too rough or choppy.	Relax. Make your moves fast and smooth.
String knots up when trick is over.	You're making triangle design wrong.	Try making the design with a yo-yo that is "dead"—or not spinning.
	···· OR ····	
	In-and-out motion is wrong.	If yo-yo starts to swing from the front, it must exit from the front. If it starts to swing from the back, it must exit from the back.

That's the last trick. There are plenty of others to learn, but if you can do all the tricks in this book, you're well on your way to mastering the art of the yo-yo!

ABOUT THE AUTHOR

World famous yo-yo champion Larry Sayco was born in Rhode Island. As a kid, he loved sports, but was too short for basketball, too light for football, and too nervous for baseball. When he saw a yo-yo pro at a boy's club, Larry knew it was the sport for him.

After high school, Larry went to work for Duncan, the world's largest yo-yo manufacturer, and soon was touring "Around the World" for them, showing off yo-yo tricks. Later he invented and patented his very own yo-yo, the Sayco Tournament Yo-Yo. After 46 years as a yo-yo pro, Larry still loves his job.

Official
Yo-Yo Pro Certificate

We, the author and publisher of
"The Ultimate Yo-Yo Book,"
hereby recognize your outstanding
Effort and Practice toward mastering
the Spinning Art of Yo-Yo and therefore award this
Certificate to _____ *with the*
Hope that your continued Practice be further rewarded
by all who appreciate your Skill,
Talent, and Performance.

Grosset & Dunlap
Publisher

Date: _____

Gary Hayes
Author